UNIVERSAL EDITION

Alfred's Basic Piano Library

Piano

Theory Book
Level 1B

INSTRUCTIONS for USE

1. This THEORY BOOK may be assigned when the student reaches page 2 of the LESSON BOOK 1B.
2. This book is coordinated page by page with LESSON BOOK 1B, and all assignments should be made according to the instructions in the upper right hand corner of each page of the THEORY BOOK.
3. Theory lessons should be completed by the student AT HOME. All assigned pages should be checked by the teacher at the next lesson.
4. Supplementary use of FLASH CARDS (available separately) is recommended.

Second Edition
Copyright © MCMXCV by Alfred Publishing Co., Inc.

The Grand Stave

Assign with page 2 of LESSON BOOK 1B.

Piano music is written on a GRAND STAVE derived from a stave of 11 lines.

The notes are named for the first 7 letters in the alphabet, repeated over and over:

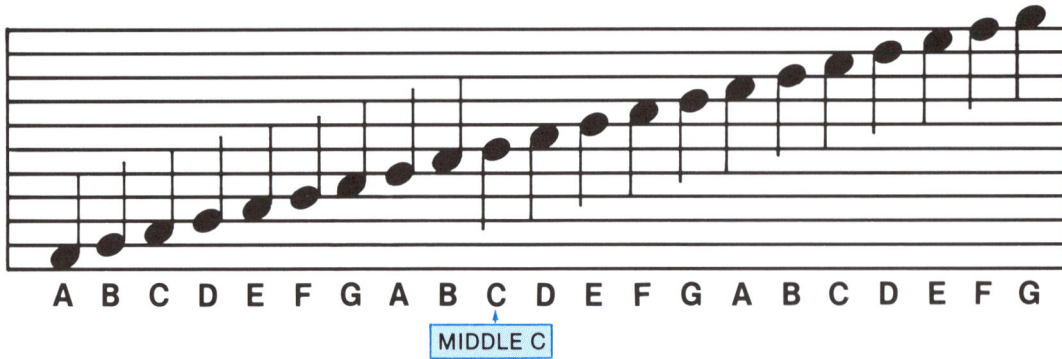

A B C D E F G A B C D E F G A B C D E F G

MIDDLE C

Since reading from so many lines would be difficult,
CLEF signs were devised to mark the F, C, and G lines:

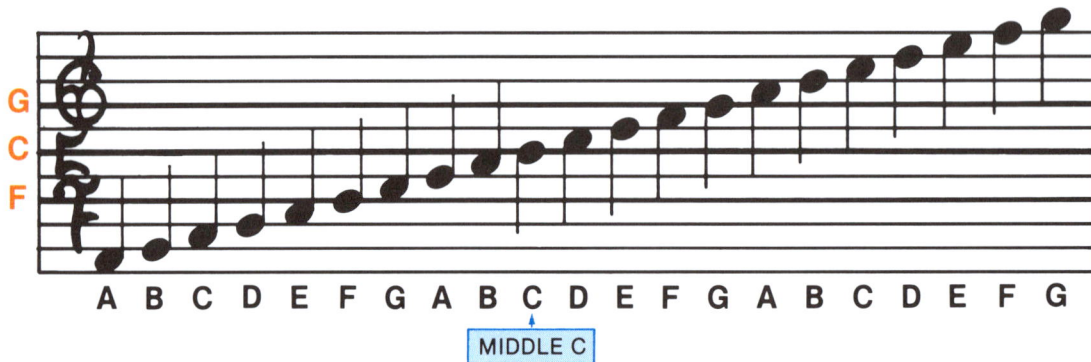

G
C
F

A B C D E F G A B C D E F G A B C D E F G

MIDDLE C

In modern music, the GRAND STAVE is separated into 2 smaller 5 line staves for easy reading.

The middle line is omitted. Instead, MIDDLE C is written on a short line,
called a LEGER line, which is added only when needed.

The F CLEF SIGN became our modern BASS CLEF SIGN 𝄢 ,
which still locates F below middle C.

The G CLEF SIGN became our modern TREBLE CLEF SIGN 𝄞 ,
which still locates G above middle C.

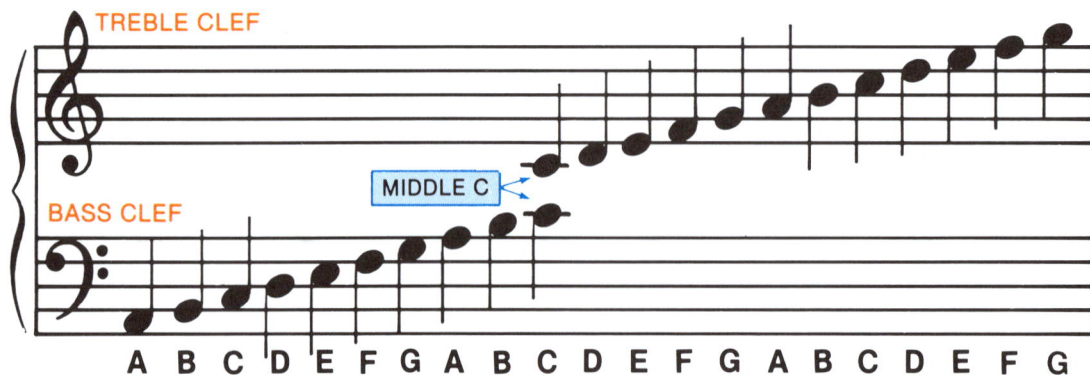

TREBLE CLEF

BASS CLEF

MIDDLE C

A B C D E F G A B C D E F G A B C D E F G

This explains why the names of the lines and spaces of the BASS STAVE are different
from those of the TREBLE STAVE. For ease in reading, it is still best to think of the GRAND STAVE
as being ONE CONTINUOUS STAVE.

Assign with page 2.

TIME SIGNATURE

$\frac{4}{4}$ means **4** beats to each bar.

$\frac{4}{4}$ a **CROTCHET** ♩ gets ONE beat.

	NOTE	REST	COUNT	TOTAL NUMBER OF COUNTS
CROTCHET	♩	𝄽	"1"	1
MINIM	𝅗𝅥	▬	"1 - 2"	2
SEMIBREVE	𝅝	▬	"1 - 2 - 3 - 4"	4

1. In the top box under each note, write the number of counts the note receives.

2. In the bottom box draw the rest that receives the same value, as shown in the 1st example.

NOTE:

TOTAL COUNTS: 4

REST:

BAR LINES divide the music into BARS. Each bar in $\frac{4}{4}$ time has notes adding up to 4 counts.

3. Complete each bar by adding just one **G** to each, so the counts in each add up to 4:

4. Complete each bar by adding just one **C** to each, so the counts in each add up to 4:

5. Complete each bar by adding just one **F** to each, so the counts in each add up to 4:

Assign with page 3.

Reviewing C Position

L.H.   **R.H.**

C D E F G   C D E F G

R.H.   1   2   3   4   5

do rei mi fa sol

do rei mi

L.H.   5   4   3   2   1

1. On the next two lines, draw BAR LINES to divide the music into bars.
   Use a DOUBLE BAR at the end of each line.

2. Write the names of the notes in the boxes.

G G F E D   C   D E F G   C

F E D   C D E F G   E D C E C

3. Write the notes that spell these words. Use CROTCHET, MINIM, or SEMIBREVE notes
   so the notes in each bar add up to 4 counts.

E D G E F E D E G G D E C K

4. Spell the same words in the BASS CLEF. The counts in each bar must add up to 4.

E D G E F E D E G G D E C K

Reviewing Melodic Intervals

Assign with page 4.

Distances between tones are measured in INTERVALS. Notes played SEPARATELY make MELODIC INTERVALS.

2nd **3rd** **4th** **5th**

Neighbouring white keys. Skip 1 white key. Skip 2 white keys. Skip 3 white keys.

2nds go from LINE to SPACE: or from SPACE to LINE:

3rds go from LINE to LINE: or from SPACE to SPACE:

4ths go from LINE to SPACE: or from SPACE to LINE:

5ths go from LINE to LINE: or from SPACE to SPACE:

1. Identify these intervals. If the interval moves UP, write UP in the top box. If it moves DOWN, write DOWN in the top box. Write the name of the interval in the lower box, as shown in the first 2 examples. If the note does not move up or down, write "SAME NOTE."

UP a 2nd | DOWN a 3rd | UP #4 | Down 5 | up 5 | Down 4

UP 3 | Down 2 | UP 2 | Down 2 | UP 3 | Down 4

UP 5 | Down 5 | UP 4 | Down 4 | UP 2 | Same Note 1

Assign with page 5.

Reviewing Rests

Look!
No Hands!

This piece should be very easy to play. Could YOU play it without a mistake?
Be careful! There is already a MISTAKE IN EVERY BAR in either the treble or bass stave.

1. CORRECT EACH MISTAKE by writing exactly ONE REST in each incomplete bar.

Very softly

Reviewing Slurs, Phrases, Legato

A **SLUR** over or under a group of notes means they are played **LEGATO** (smoothly connected).

SLURS often divide the music into **PHRASES** (musical thoughts or sentences).
Notice how the following slurs separate the question from the answer, and at the same time show that they are played LEGATO:

mf
How   are   you   to - day?   I   am   feel - ing   fine.

2. Play the above line of music.
    - Be sure to play LEGATO.

    - Lift at the end of each phrase, just after you count "1-2-3-4" for the
      semibreves. This lift should be like taking a slight breath at the end
      of the question and at the end of the answer, without adding any time
      to the value of the notes.

Reviewing Dynamics: *mf*, *f*, & *p*

3. Write the correct dynamic sign in each empty box:

LOUD		MODERATELY LOUD		SOFT	

The Boy and the Echo

Assign with page 5.

C POSITION

1. Each phrase in this piece should be marked with a SLUR. ADD THE MISSING SLURS.
2. The L.H. phrases (THE BOY) should be *forte*. Add an *f* under the 1st note of each L.H. phrase.
3. The R.H. phrases (THE ECHO) should be *piano*. Add a *p* under the 1st note of each R.H. phrase.

Now that you have completed THE BOY AND THE ECHO, you will find that it is a good RECITAL PIECE.

4. Play THE BOY AND THE ECHO. Make up some more phrases for the echo to answer, if you wish. You can't play anything that sounds wrong if you stay in C POSITION and answer each phrase with the same notes played by the R.H. Always end with the last 5 bars, as written above.

8

Reviewing Harmonic Intervals

Assign with page 6.

Notes played together make **HARMONIC INTERVALS.**

1. Play these HARMONIC INTERVALS, saying the names aloud:

2. In the upper boxes, write the names of the notes that complete these HARMONIC INTERVALS:

| 2nd | D / C | 2nd | E / D | 2nd | F / E | 2nd | G / F | 3rd | E / C |
| 3rd | F / D | 3rd | G / E | 4th | F / C | 4th | G / D | 5th | G / C |

Reviewing $\frac{3}{4}$ Time *Assign with page 7.*

$\frac{3}{4}$ means **3** beats to each bar.

a **CROTCHET** ♩ gets ONE beat.

♩. = DOTTED MINIM

COUNT: "1 - 2 - 3"

Day is Done

1. Write the names of the HARMONIC INTERVALS in the boxes.
2. Play & count.

5   3   5   3   4   2   3

p Slow - ly,   slow - ly,   Sinks   the   sun.

5   3   5   3   4   2   3

p Night   is   fall - ing,   Day   is   done.

Reviewing the Sharp Sign

The **SHARP SIGN** before a note means play the next key to the RIGHT, whether black or white!

The SHARP SIGN before a note applies to that note each time it appears in the same bar.

A Sharp Song

1. In the 1st bar below, is the 4th note a sharp note? Answer:_____ .
2. Write the names of the notes in the boxes.
3. Play and say the note names: "A SHARP," etc.

Moderately slow

Here's a song that's ver - y sharp, You don't play an - y white keys! Just

keep your fin - gers on the blacks, and you will play the right keys!

10

Assign with page 9.

Reviewing Staccato

STACCATO is the opposite of LEGATO.
It means SEPARATED or DETACHED.
To play STACCATO, release the key instantly.

STACCATO is indicated by a DOT over

or under the note.

When you play staccato, move the hand UP immediately after touching the key!

HAND POSITION
for the music on this page.

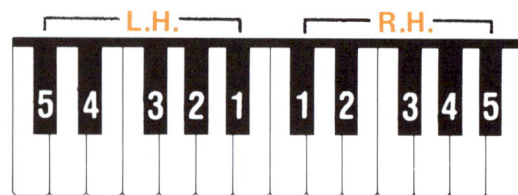

Meat-Ball Polka

1. Add staccato dots over or under the CROTCHETS.
   If the stems point UP, put the dot BELOW the note-head.
   If the stems point DOWN, put the dot ABOVE the note-head.

2. Play MEAT-BALL POLKA. Carefully observe the staccato marks.

Moderately fast

One meat-ball! / That is all / Ma - ma cooked for / din - ner!
That is all! / One meat-ball! / Pa - pa's get - ting / thin - ner!

Reviewing Incomplete Bars

Assign with pages 10–11.

When a piece begins with an INCOMPLETE BAR, the counts missing
in the FIRST BAR are found in the LAST BAR.

Cowboy Song

3. Add the missing BAR LINES. The counts in the LAST BAR plus the FIRST BAR
   should equal ONE FULL BAR.

4. Play COWBOY SONG & COUNT! Be sure to repeat.

Moderately Slow

1. I'm just a poor cow - boy, a long way from home.
2. All night on the prai - rie I ride and I roam.

Reviewing G Position

The Band-Leader

1. Write the names of the notes in the boxes.   2. Play.

Moderately fast, like a march.

| D | B | G | A | B | C | D |

f

1. I'm the lead-er of the band. Out in front I proud-ly stand.
2. I just have to wave my hand; Out comes mu-sic, loud and grand!

| D | C | B | A | G | B | G |

3. Write notes from the G POSITION that spell these words. Use CROTCHET, MINIM, DOTTED MINIM, or SEMIBREVE notes so the notes in each bar add up to 4 counts.

G A B   D A B   B A G   D A D

4. Write the notes that spell these words in the TREBLE CLEF. The counts in each bar must add up to 4.

G A D   B A D   C A B   A D D

Reviewing the Flat Sign

Assign with page 15.

The **FLAT SIGN** before a note means play the next key to the LEFT, whether black or white.

G♭

G

L.H.   R.H.

G♭ A♭ B♭ D♭ E♭   G♭ A♭ B♭ D♭ E♭
G A B C D E   G A B C D E

R.H. 1 2 3 4 5

L.H. 5 4 3 2 1

The FLAT SIGN before a note applies to that note each time it appears in the same bar.

REVIEW: DYNAMIC SIGNS

CRESCENDO (gradually louder)   DIMINUENDO (gradually softer)

Our Car Has 5 Flats

1. Write the names of the notes in the boxes.
2. Play and say the note names: "G FLAT," etc.

G♭ A♭ B♭ D♭   E♭ D♭ B♭ A♭   G♭

Sadly!

mf

1. Our car has 5 flats, and that's not fair!
2. 2 in front, plus 2 in back and spare.

p

All our tyres keep run-ning out of air.
I don't think we're go-ing an-y-where!

mf

G♭ A♭ B♭ D♭   E♭ D♭ B♭ A♭   G♭

Reviewing Middle C Position

Assign with page 16.

Prelude on Middle C

This is an attractive RECITAL PIECE!

1. Write the note names in the boxes.
2. Play.

Moderately fast

Tempo Marks

Assign with pages 17–18.

The following Italian words are *tempo marks.* They tell how fast or slow to play.

ALLEGRO = Quickly, happily.   **ANDANTE** = Moving along ("walking").   **ADAGIO** = Slowly.
MODERATO = Moderately. The word Moderato is sometimes used with one of the other words.
Example: Allegro moderato = moderately fast.

Three Short Pieces in MIDDLE C POSITION

1. Read the words to each of these 3 short pieces, then decide on the best TEMPO marks and DYNAMIC signs and ADD THEM.

2. Add bar lines.

3. At the end of each piece, add a sign that means REPEAT.

4. Play the pieces.

1. Hap - pi - ly,   hap - pi - ly,   run - ning a - long!
2. Mer - ri - ly,   mer - ri - ly,   sing - ing this song!

1. Slow - ly the   clouds go   drift - ing   by.
2. Slow - ly they   sail   a - cross the   sky.

1. Let's   go   strol - ling   lei - sure - ly.
2. On   the   beach   be - side the   sea.

Pauses Are to Hold!

A note under a **PAUSE** ⌒ is held longer than its value.

1. Write the names of the notes in the boxes below.
2. Play. Hold the notes with the pauses longer than their values.
3. Play & say or sing the words.
4. How many pause signs are in this piece? _____

Pauses and Rainbows

MIDDLE C POSITION

Moderato

1. It is a pause sign, And it's a hold sign.
2. When moth-er held me, I'd see a rain - bow.

They look like rain bows; I'll tell you why:_____
She made my world glow; I'd nev - er cry!

Assign with page 21.

Quavers

ONE CROTCHET = TWO QUAVERS

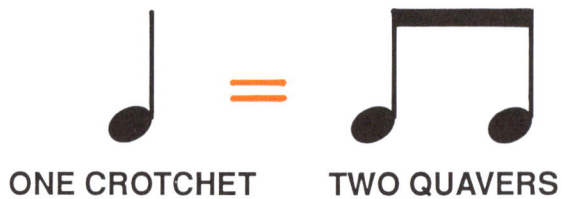

QUAVERS are usually played in PAIRS. They are joined together with a BEAM:

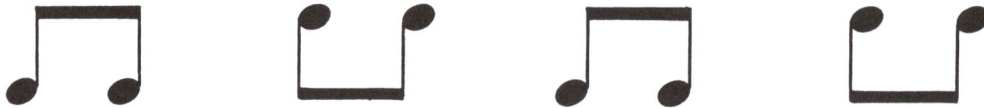

1. Change these crotchets to QUAVERS by adding a BEAM to each pair:

To count music containing quavers, divide each beat into 2 parts:

count: "one-and" for each crotchet;

count: "one-and" for each pair of quavers.

2. Play the following while you count aloud: "One-and, one-and," etc.

MIDDLE C POSITION

COUNT: One - and, one - and, one - and, One - and, one - and, one - and.

COUNT: One - and, one - and, one - and, One - and, one - and, one - and.

3. Write one note equal to the sum of each pair of tied notes:

Assign with page 22.

$\frac{2}{4}$ means **2** beats to each bar.

$\frac{2}{4}$ a **crotchet** gets one beat.

Kookaburra

1. Add bar lines.
2. Play. Observe the accent sign >, which means play that one note or chord LOUDER.

Allegro moderato

A semibreve rest is used to indicate a whole bar of silence in $\frac{2}{4}$ time.

Koo - ka - bur - ra sits on an old gum tree, Mer - ry, mer - ry

king of the bush is he, Laugh, Koo - ka - bur - ra,

Laugh, Koo-ka-bur-ra, Gay your life must be! Whee!

3. In the three lines below, add time signatures at the beginning of each line.
4. Clap (or tap) the rhythm of each line, counting aloud.
5. Say the words of each line in rhythm.

Boots! Boots! March - ing up and down a - gain!

We wish you a Mer - ry Christ - mas, and a Hap - py New Year!

Oh, I went down South for to see my gal sing-ing pol-ly wol-ly doo-dle all day.

How's Your Italian?

Assign with pages 23–24.

Many Italian terms are used in music in almost every country in the world.
You have learned a lot of them already. Let's see how much Italian you now know.

Draw lines connecting the dots on the matching boxes.

TEMPO	slow
RITARDANDO	rate of speed
ADAGIO	slowing down
ANDANTE	moderate speed
MODERATO	walking speed
ALLEGRO	from the beginning
Da CAPO	fast
FINE	gradually louder
CRESCENDO	the end
DIMINUENDO	moderately loud
MEZZO FORTE	gradually softer
PIANO	loud
FORTE	soft
LEGATO	detached
STACCATO	return to original speed
A TEMPO	smoothly connected

G Positions for L.H.

Old Position   New Position

G A B C D   G A B C D

L.H. 5 4 3 2 1   5 4 3 2 1

The Big Rock Candy Mountain

1. Write the note names in the boxes ABOVE the notes. This will help you learn the NEW G POSITION.
2. Write the note names in the boxes BELOW the notes. This reviews the old G POSITION.
3. Play & count.
4. Play and say or sing the words.

Allegro

B C D D C B C D D C B C

mf

There's a gum - drop tree, and a milk - shake sea, and a

D D A C B G

And the pump - kin pies grow to

so - da wa - ter foun - tain,

B C D D C B C

mon - strous size in the Big Rock Can - dy Moun - tain!

D D C B C D D A C B G

The Damper Pedal

Assign with pages 26–31.

Use the RIGHT FOOT on the RIGHT PEDAL, called the **DAMPER PEDAL.**

This sign shows when the damper pedal is to be used:

Pedal down   hold pedal   Pedal up

THE DAMPER PEDAL

The music on this page helps you to develop freedom of movement at the keyboard.

The hands play in a new position in each measure. L.H. & R.H. play in either clef.

You will learn how the pedal connects the notes together, LEGATO,
even while the hands are changing positions.

G-B-D-F's

The 1st note of each bar is G. The notes of each bar are a 3rd apart.

1. Write the names of the notes in the boxes.
2. Play. Stems down = L.H. Stems up = R.H. Hold the pedal down through the entire line.

A-C-E-G's

The 1st note of each bar is A. The notes in each bar are a 3rd apart.

3. Write the names of the notes in the boxes.
4. Play. Stems down = L.H. Stems up = R.H. Hold the pedal, as indicated.

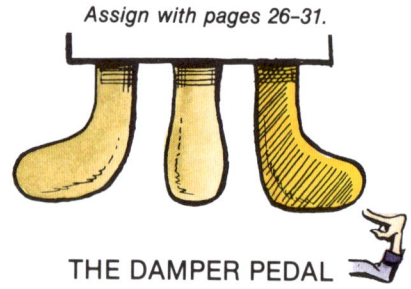

Assign with pages 32–33.

More About Quavers

♩ This is a **QUAVER REST.**
It means REST FOR THE VALUE OF A QUAVER.

Pairs of QUAVERS are joined with a beam: ♫ or

Single QUAVERS have a FLAG instead of a beam: ♪ or

1. Make these crotchets into SINGLE-QUAVERS. Trace the 1st tail,
   then add tails to the other notes.

2. Trace the 1st QUAVER REST, then draw quaver rests between the other notes.

| Quaver | Quaver Rest | Quaver | Quaver Rest | Quaver | Quaver Rest | Quaver | Quaver Rest | Quaver |

Reviewing Note & Rest Values

QUAVER = ♪   CROTCHET = ♩   MINIM = ♩   SEMIBREVE = 𝅝

QUAVER REST = ♩   CROTCHET REST = 𝄽   MINIM REST = ▃
(sits on line)   SEMIBREVE REST = ▀
(hangs down)

A SEMIBREVE REST is also used to indicate silence for any WHOLE BAR of $\frac{2}{4}$, $\frac{3}{4}$, or $\frac{4}{4}$!

3. Complete these bars by adding only ONE REST to each bar.

$\frac{2}{4}$

$\frac{3}{4}$

$\frac{4}{4}$

Middle D Position

Assign with pages 34-35.

L.H. R.H.

G A B C **D** E F G A

R.H. 1 2 3 4 5

BOTH THUMBS on MIDDLE D!

L.H. 5 4 3 2 1

O Bury Me Not on the Lone Prairie

1. Write the names of the notes in the boxes.
2. Play.

Moderato

mf

1. "O   bur - y   me   not _____   on the lone   prai -
2. From   pale and dry   lips _____   of a youth who

5

2

rie!" _____   These   words   came   low _____
lay _____   Up - on   came   his   bed _____

4

and — mourn - ful - ly, ——————
at the close of day. ————————

Note Review *Assign with page 35.*

NOTES ON LINES:

<u>G</u> <u>B</u> <u>D</u> <u>F</u> <u>A</u> <u>C</u> <u>E</u> <u>G</u> <u>B</u> <u>D</u> <u>F</u>

NOTES IN SPACES:

<u>A</u> <u>C</u> <u>E</u> <u>G</u> <u>B</u> <u>D</u> <u>F</u> <u>A</u> <u>C</u> <u>E</u>

1. Write the names of the notes in the boxes.
2. Play. Use L.H. 3 for notes below middle C. Use R.H. 3 for notes on or above middle C.

Semitones

Assign with pages 36–37.

A **SEMITONE** or **HALF STEP** is the distance from any key
to the very next key above or below,
whether black or white.

SEMITONES • NO KEY BETWEEN

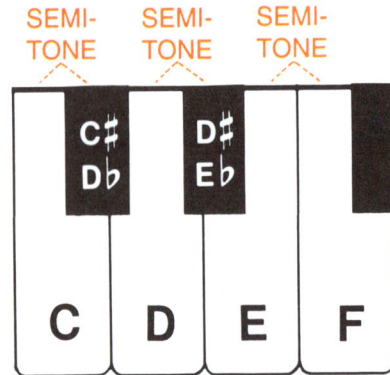

SEMI-TONE SEMI-TONE SEMI-TONE

C# Db   D# Eb

C D E F

The SHARP sign ♯ raises a note a semitone (play next key to the right).

The FLAT sign ♭ lowers a note a semitone (play the next key to the left).

The NATURAL sign ♮ cancels a sharp or flat!

1. Make some NATURAL SIGNS. Trace the 1st sign, then draw 6 more.

EACH BLACK KEY MAY BE NAMED 2 WAYS. EXAMPLE: **C♯ = D♭**

THESE WHITE KEYS MAY ALSO BE NAMED 2 WAYS: **C = B♯ F = E♯ B = C♭ E = F♭**

2. Write 2 different names for each indicated key, as shown in the first 2 examples:

C# E#
Db F

Assign with page 38.

Whole Tones

A **WHOLE TONE** or **WHOLE STEP**
is equal to 2 semitones.
Skip one key…black or white.

WHOLE TONES • ONE KEY BETWEEN

WHOLE TONE WHOLE TONE WHOLE TONE WHOLE TONE WHOLE TONE

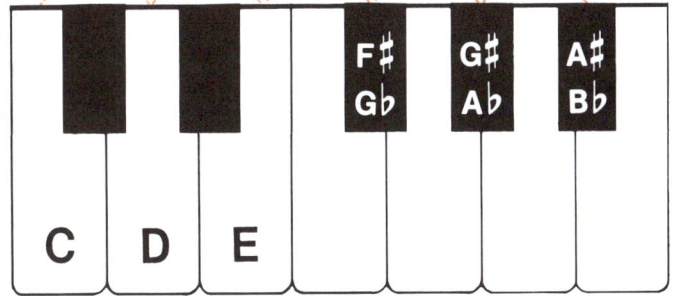

1. Write the names on the keys, continuing up the keyboard in **WHOLE TONES.**
   Use SHARPS for the black keys.

2. Write the names on the keys, continuing up the keyboard in **WHOLE TONES.**
   Use FLATS for the black keys.

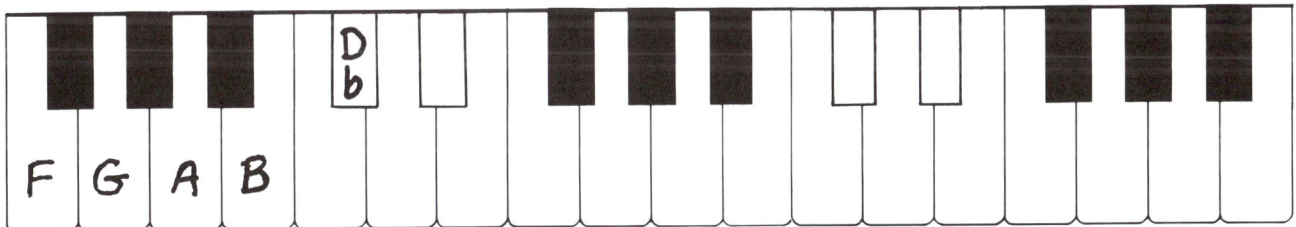

3. In the following squares write ½ for each **SEMITONE** and 1 for each **WHOLE TONE**
   indicated by the arrows.

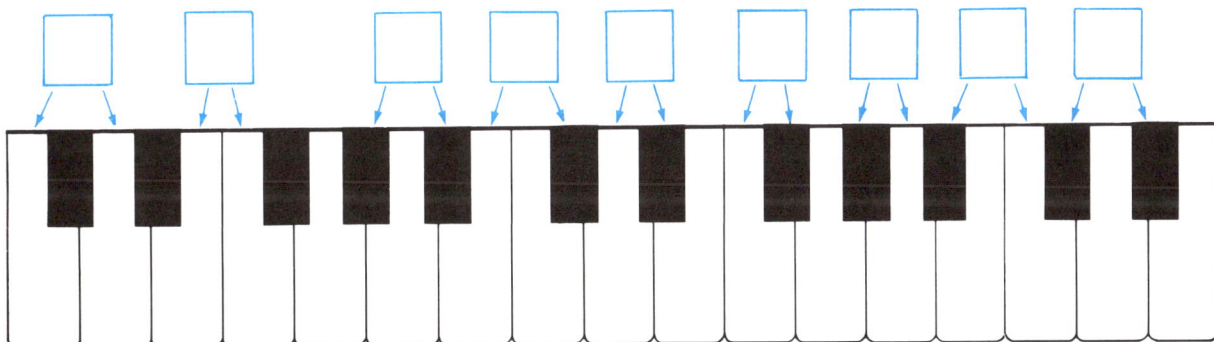

Steps to Progress

Assign with page 39.

Get everything on this page correct and you will never have trouble with SEMITONES & WHOLE TONES!

1. Write ½ for each SEMITONE and 1 for each WHOLE TONE:

Some tricky ones:

2. Change the following SEMITONES to WHOLE TONES by adding one accidental (♯, ♭, or ♮) before the 2nd note of each bar.

3. Change the following WHOLE TONES to SEMITONES by adding one accidental before the 2nd note of each bar.

Assign with page 40.

Tetrachords

A **TETRACHORD** is a series of **FOUR NOTES** having a pattern of
WHOLE TONE, WHOLE TONE, SEMITONE.

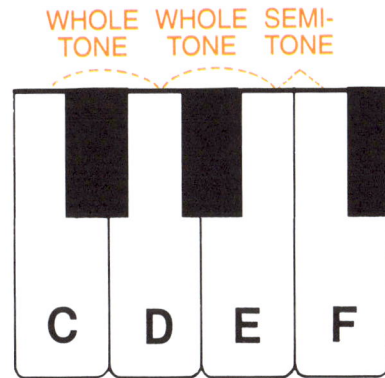

WHOLE   WHOLE   SEMI-
TONE   TONE   TONE

C D E F

The four notes of a tetrachord must always be
NEIGHBOURING LETTERS of the **MUSICAL ALPHABET.**

1. Study the following 4 TETRACHORDS and answer these questions:
   - Does each consist of WHOLE TONE, WHOLE TONE, SEMITONE? Answer: _____.
   - Are the notes of each tetrachord NEIGHBOURING LETTERS OF THE MUSICAL ALPHABET?
     Answer:_____
   - Underline the correct spelling of the **D** tetrachord: **D E G♭G   D E F♯G**
   - Underline the correct spelling of the **A** tetrachord: **A B D♭D   A B C♯D**

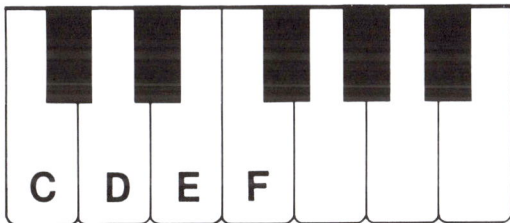

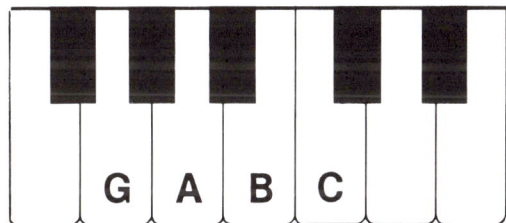

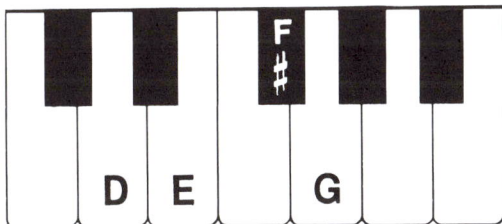

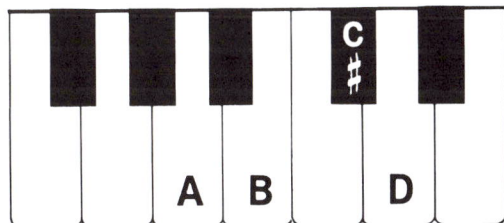

C D E F   G A B C

F♯   C♯
D E G   A B D

2. Write tetrachords beginning on each of the following notes:

The Major Scale

Assign with page 41.

The **MAJOR SCALE** is made of **TWO TETRACHORDS** joined by a whole tone.

1. Write the letter names of the notes of the C MAJOR SCALE on the keyboard below.
2. Play the 1st tetrachord with L.H. 5 4 3 2, and the 2nd tetrachord with R.H. 2 3 4 5.

THE C MAJOR
SCALE

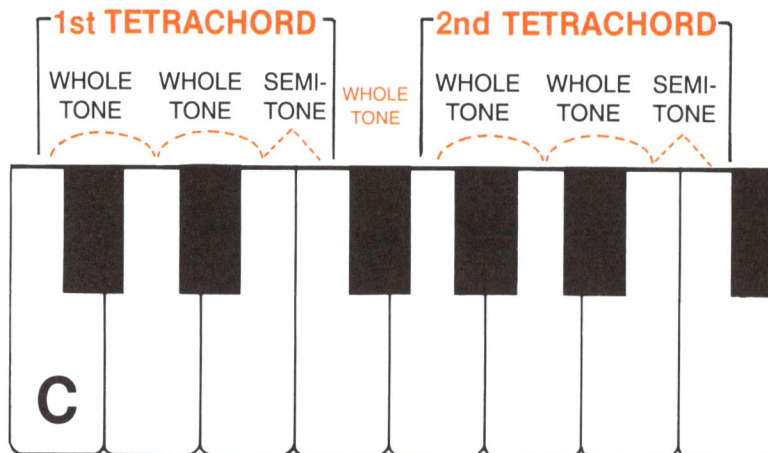

1st TETRACHORD

WHOLE TONE   WHOLE TONE   SEMI-TONE

WHOLE TONE

2nd TETRACHORD

WHOLE TONE   WHOLE TONE   SEMI-TONE

C

3. Write the letter names of the notes of the G MAJOR SCALE on the keyboard below.
4. Play the 1st tetrachord with L.H. 5 4 3 2, and the 2nd tetrachord with R.H. 2 3 4 5.

THE G MAJOR
SCALE

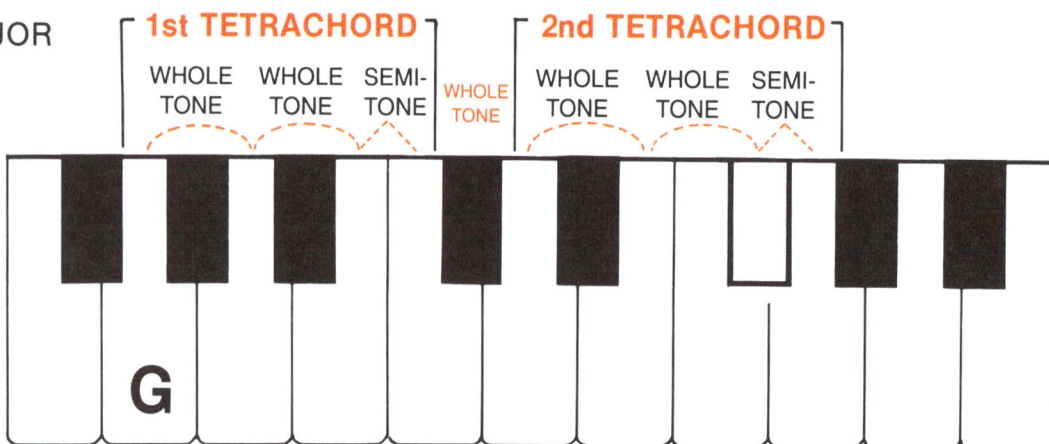

1st TETRACHORD

WHOLE TONE   WHOLE TONE   SEMI-TONE

WHOLE TONE

2nd TETRACHORD

WHOLE TONE   WHOLE TONE   SEMI-TONE

G

5. Write tetrachords beginning on each of the following notes.
6. Play as follows: 1st tetrachord with L.H. 5 4 3 2, 2nd with R.H. 2 3 4 5.

   2nd tetrachord with L.H. 5 4 3 2, 3rd with R.H. 2 3 4 5.

   3rd tetrachord with L.H. 5 4 3 2, 4th with R.H. 2 3 4 5.

The Key of G Major

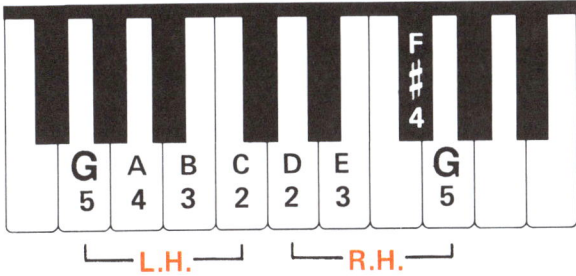

Assign with page 42.

The G MAJOR SCALE has ONE SHARP, F♯.

A piece based on the G MAJOR SCALE is in the **KEY OF G MAJOR.**

Instead of placing a ♯ before every **F** in the piece,
the ♯ is indicated at the beginning, in the **KEY SIGNATURE.**

**SHARPS OR FLATS GIVEN IN THE KEY SIGNATURE.
ARE EFFECTIVE THROUGHOUT THE PIECE.**

1. Draw a circle around the notes that are made ♯ by the key signatures.

2. Play both G major scales.

KEY SIGNATURE:
One sharp (F♯)

KEY SIGNATURE:
One sharp (F♯)

Sea Shanty

1. The key signature applies to all F's, on ANY line or space.
   Circle the notes affected by the key signature.

2. Play. Use the G TETRACHORD POSITION shown
   at the top of this page.

Allegro moderato

1. 'Twas a Fri - day morn when we ___ set ___
2. When the Cap - tain spied a fair ___ mer -

sail, And we were not far from the land, ___
maid, With a comb and glass in her hand. ___

Music with 2 L.H. Positions

Assign with page 43.

SOME PIECES KEEP THE R.H. POSITION THROUGHOUT, BUT CHANGE L.H. POSITIONS.

1. Write the name of the key played by each L.H. finger in G POSITION:

KEY: | | | | | |

| L.H. FINGER: | 5 | 4 | 3 | 2 | 1 |

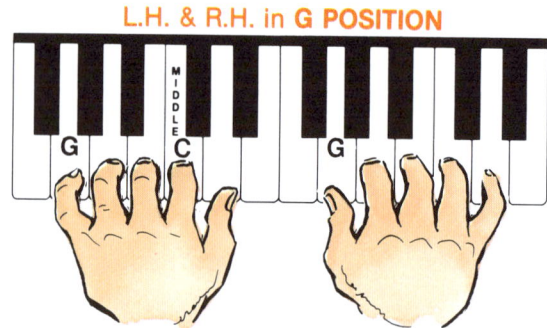

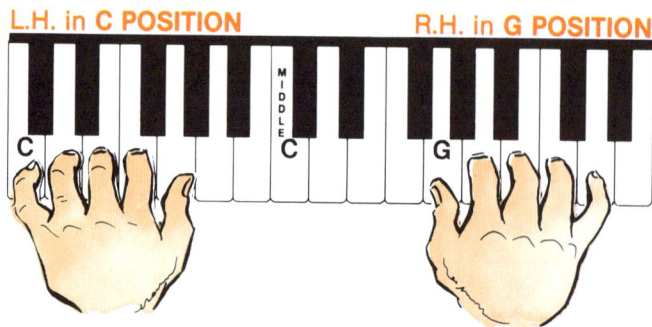

L.H. & R.H. in G POSITION

2. Write the name of the key played by each R.H. finger in G POSITION:

KEY: | | | | | |

| R.H. FINGER: | 1 | 2 | 3 | 4 | 5 |

3. Write the name of the key played by each L.H. finger in C POSITION:

KEY: | | | | | |

| L.H. FINGER: | 5 | 4 | 3 | 2 | 1 |

L.H. in C POSITION   **R.H. in G POSITION**

KEY OF C MAJOR.
KEY SIGNATURE:
No sharps, no flats.

A Merry Song

4. Look at the music and decide what positions are used for each line. Fill in the boxes.

5. Play.

R.H. = _____ POSITION

mf

1. I love to sing this mer - ry song,
2. I love to sing it all day long,
3. 'Cause when I'm sad it makes me glad!

Fid-dle did-dle dee, yup, hey!

Fine

L.H. = _____ POSITION

L.H. = _____ POSITION

I love to sing it when I'm glad; I love to sing it when I'm sad;

D.C. al Fine

L.H. = _____ POSITION

Music with 2 R.H. Positions

Assign with pages 44–45.

SOME PIECES KEEP THE L.H. POSITION THROUGHOUT, BUT CHANGE R.H. POSITIONS.

L.H. & R.H. in C POSITION

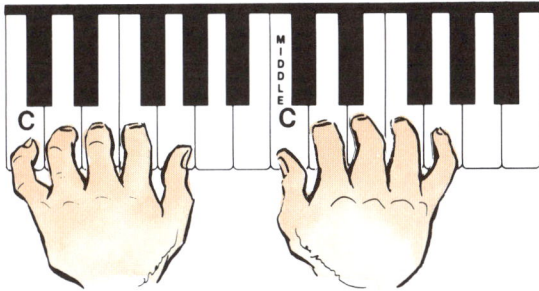

1. Write the name of the key played by each R.H. finger in C POSITION:

KEY:					
R.H. FINGER:	1	2	3	4	5

2. Write the name of the key played by each L.H. finger in the C POSITION:

KEY:					
L.H. FINGER:	5	4	3	2	1

L.H. in C POSITION   **R.H. in G POSITION**

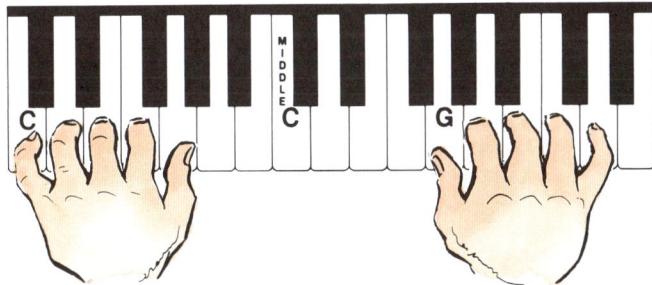

3. Write the name of the key played by each R.H. finger in G POSITION:

KEY:					
R.H. FINGER:	1	2	3	4	5

The Fox

R.H. = _____ POSITION

4. Look at the music and decide what positions are used for each line. Fill in the boxes.

5. Play.

R.H. = _____ POSITION

L.H. = _____ POSITION

mf

1. Said the fox on a star - ry night,
2. Moon and stars gon - na give me light,
3. Hope I don't get a tum - my ache,

"Go - in' to the town - O!
Go - in' to the town - O!
Go - in' to the town - O!"

Fine

p Hope I meet with the far - mer's drake, Just to greet him for old time's sake!

D.C. al Fine

Musical Draughts

Assign with page 46.

OPPONENT'S PLAYERS

YOUR PLAYERS

1. tetra-chord
2. equal to 𝅝
3. semi-tone
4. whole tone
5. equal to 𝅗𝅥.
6. 5th
7. 4th
8. 3rd
9. equal to 𝅘𝅥
10. key signature: G MAJOR
11. same as
12. same as

HOW TO PLAY:

The circles on the bottom 3 rows of the board are your "players." Begin with your player 1. Find the matching player on your opponent's side (top 3 rows). Write "1" at the top of the opponent's player, then draw a diagonal line through that square (see example below). Continue to 2, etc. Each time you put one of YOUR numbers on one of the opponent's players, you "capture" that player. When you capture them all, you win the game!

TO CAPTURE A PLAYER:

*Write your number on
the opponent's matching player.
Draw a diagonal line through
the opponent's square.*